AUSTRALIA & ANTARCTICA

Island Continents & Supercontinents

Continents

Bruce McClish

First published 2003 by Heinemann Library
a division of Harcourt Education Australia,
18–22 Salmon Street, Port Melbourne Victoria 3207 Australia
(a division of Reed International Books Australia Pty Ltd, ABN 70 001 002 357).
Visit the Heinemann Library website at www.heinemannlibrary.com.au

⟨ℛ⟩ A Reed Elsevier company

Editor: Carmel Heron
Designer: Stella Vassiliou
Photo researcher: Margaret Maher
Production controller: Chris Roberts
Maps and diagrams by Pat Kermode and Stella Vassiliou

Typeset in Palatino 13/18pt by Stella Vassiliou
Film separations by Digital Imaging Group (DIG), Melbourne
Printed in China by Wing King Tong Co. Ltd.

National Library of Australia
Cataloguing-in-Publication data:

McClish, Bruce.
  Australia & Antarctica: island continents & supercontinents.

  Bibliography.
  Includes index.
  ISBN 1 74070 129 1

  1. Continents – Juvenile literature. 2. Islands – Juvenile literature. 3. Australia – Juvenile literature. 4. Antarctica – Juvenile literature. I. Title. (Series : McClish, Bruce. Continents).

994

The author would like to thank: Avi Olshina, geologist, Victorian Government; Peter Nunan, geography teacher, Royal Geographical Society of Queensland; Craig Campbell, researcher; Jenny McClish, researcher and contributing author.

Main cover image of outback New South Wales, Australia, supplied by Tourism New South Wales. Other images supplied by: Auscape/Jean-Paul Ferrero: pp. 17, 19, 22, /Dennis Harding: p. 26; ANT Photo Library/Jonathan Chester: p. 18 (top); Australian Picture Library: p. 15; Coo-ee Picture Library: p. 25 (left); Greening Australia: p. 29; Rod Ledingham: p. 16; By permission of the National Library of Australia: p. 21; © Natural History Museum (London): p. 25 (right); Nature Focus/Carl Bento: p. 28; Not Bad Design & Print, www.notbad.com.au: p. 12; PhotoDisc: pp. 5, 11 (left), 18 (bottom); Tourism New South Wales: pp. 7 (all), 9, 27; Tourism Victoria: p. 8.

Contents

Island
CONTINENTS

A continent is a huge **landmass** on the surface of the Earth. We generally speak of seven continents: Europe, Asia, Africa, North America, South America, Australia and Antarctica.

Most continents lie near – or are actually connected to – some other continent. For example, Europe lies near Africa, and North America is connected to South America. There are only two continents that are isolated from all the others, completely surrounded by seas. These are the island continents, Australia and Antarctica.

In some ways, Australia and Antarctica seem very different from each other. One continent is known for hot deserts and sunny beaches, while the other is known for massive **glaciers** and frozen seas. Yet aside from **climate**, Australia and Antarctica have a lot in common. Both are among the smaller-sized continents (which also include Europe). Besides being the only island continents, they are the only continents that lie completely in the **Southern Hemisphere** (with seasons reversed from those of the **Northern Hemisphere**). They were also the last continents to be explored and occupied by Europeans.

The Gondwana connection

Australia and Antarctica are island continents today. However, millions of years ago they were connected to each other. At one time, they were also part of a massive supercontinent called Gondwana. This supercontinent was made up of other huge landmasses, including Africa, India and South America. In ancient times, plants and animals from Australia could easily spread into Antarctica – as well as many other parts of Gondwana.

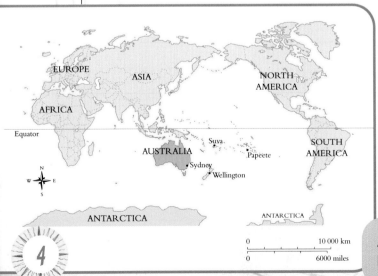

EUROPE
ASIA
NORTH AMERICA
AFRICA
Equator
AUSTRALIA
Suva
Papeete
SOUTH AMERICA
Sydney
Wellington
N W E S
ANTARCTICA
ANTARCTICA

| 0 | 10 000 km |
| 0 | 6000 miles |

Australia and Antarctica are known as the island continents.

About 200 million years ago, Gondwana began to break up. Forces from deep within the Earth caused different parts of the supercontinent to move slowly apart. Because of this movement, Australia and Antarctica both became separated and isolated. While continents such as Africa and South America eventually moved closer to other continents, Australia and Antarctica were in remote parts of the ocean. Australia moved north towards the warm **equator**. Antarctica remained close to the South Pole. Despite their isolation today, Australia and Antarctica still share certain kinds of wildlife, such as penguins.

The thousands of islands in the central and southern Pacific are known as Oceania. This includes places such as New Caledonia, Tonga, Samoa, Vanuatu and Fiji. Some **geographers** say that Australia is part of Oceania too, along with Papua New Guinea and New Zealand. The total land area of this larger Oceania covers more than 8 500 000 square kilometres. Some geographers also believe Oceania should be considered a continent, with Australia as its largest island. Yet Australia is by far the greatest part of Oceania, covering more than 90 per cent of its and surface.

Different kinds of penguins live in Australia and Antarctica, as well as on the coasts and islands of South America and Africa.

Introducing
AUSTRALIA

Australia is the smallest and flattest continent. It is the only continent that is also a country, with the entire **landmass** controlled by one government.

The name 'Australia' comes from the Latin word *australis*, which means 'southern'. The English nicknamed Australia 'the land down under', because it is in such a southerly position. The word 'Australasia' is sometimes used to include Australia, New Zealand and certain Pacific islands.

Most of Australia is dry and thinly populated. Shortage of water is often a problem. Even so, Australia's coastal areas can be quite green and **fertile**, especially in the south-east. The largest cities are also in these coastal regions.

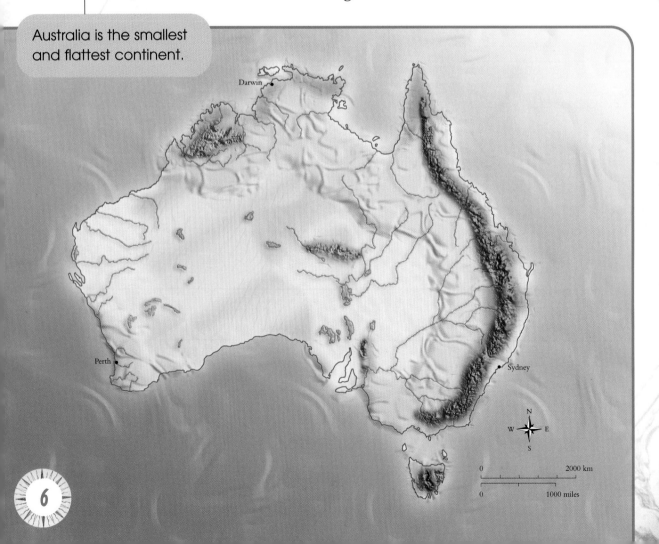

Australia is the smallest and flattest continent.

Australia has a surprising variety of scenery, including snowy mountains, lush rainforests, sandy beaches and the world's longest chain of coral reefs and islands – the Great Barrier Reef. Australian animals, such as the platypus, kangaroo and koala, are unlike those of any other continent.

Australia is a prosperous land, with productive industries such as farming, mining and tourism. Most of the people have a high **standard of living**.

Area: 7 682 300 sq km

Climate: temperate and tropical

Population: 19 231 000 (estimated 2002)

Highest peak: Mt Kosciusko (2228 metres above sea level)

Lowest point: Lake Eyre (16 metres below sea level)

Largest lake (salt): Lake Eyre (9000 sq km)

Longest river: Murray–Darling river system (3750 km)

Biggest desert: Great Victoria Desert (388 500 sq km)

Crop products: wheat, fruits, sugar, barley, oats, rice, vegetables, cotton, **timber**

Animals and animal products: sheep and wool, cattle (beef and dairy), chickens and eggs, fish and shellfish

Mineral products: copper, gold, lead, silver, iron ore, zinc, nickel, bauxite, manganese, coal, natural gas, petroleum, titanium, zircon, uranium

Other products and industries: electrical equipment, clothing and textiles, **pharmaceuticals**, chemicals, steel, automobiles, aircraft, ships, processed food, paper, tourism

Australia has productive farming industries.

Most Australians can enjoy sunny weather and outdoor recreation throughout the year.

Land and landforms

Much of the Australian land surface is very old and worn. There are mountains, but few of them are very high. Australia is the only continent without **glaciers** or an active volcano.

Mountains

Australia's biggest mountains lie along the east coast. The Great Dividing Range – also called the Great Divide – is the continent's longest and highest mountain chain. It reaches from the northern tip of Queensland all the way into southern Victoria. Mt Kosciusko, Australia's highest mountain, is part of the Great Dividing Range. Many slopes of this range are covered with forests and woodlands. In the southern part, there are **alpine** meadows and winter snowfields. Similar mountain ranges can be found in Tasmania.

West of the Great Dividing Range, and across most of the continent, the land is low and flat. There are some mountains here, but they are not very high when compared with larger mountains of other continents. Millions of years ago, these Australian mountains were much higher, but they were gradually worn down by **erosion**.

The Central Lowlands

There are plains on most coastal areas of Australia. But much wider and lower plains are in the Central Lowlands of Australia. The Central Lowlands lie east of the Great Dividing Range and extend into central Australia. This area is dry most of the year, with immense regions of desert, scrub and salt lakes. There are no large cities in the Central Lowlands.

The mountain range of the Grampions, in central-west Victoria.

Ancient landscapes

Most of central and Western Australia is covered with a very ancient rock surface. Some of these rocks are billions of years old. Although much of the land is flat and dry, it is higher in **elevation** than the Central Lowlands, with many hills and low mountains. Central and Western Australia are important regions for mining and cattle grazing.

Rivers and water

Rivers are important in a dry continent such as Australia. Rivers on the eastern side of the Great Dividing Range generally flow a short distance before emptying into the sea. Rivers on the western side, including the Murray and the Darling, can flow for thousands of kilometres across the dry plains. Most of these rivers do not flow during the dry season.

Australia has great natural stores of underground water. This comes in handy in dry areas without a river, especially for **livestock**. The underground water can be pumped (or sometimes flows naturally) to the surface.

Diary of a continent

▶ **280 million years ago**
Much of Australia is covered with glaciers in a great southern **ice age**.

▶ **200 million years ago**
Australia is part of the Gondwana supercontinent, along with Antarctica, Africa and South America.

▶ **150 million years ago**
Gondwana breaks up.

▶ **100 million years ago**
Central Australia is flooded by seas during the **Age of Reptiles**.

▶ **40 million years ago**
Australia tears away from Antarctica and begins to drift north.

▶ **60 000–40 000 years ago**
Humans cross a **land bridge** from Papua New Guinea to inhabit Australia.

▶ **1788**
Europeans start permanent settlement in Australia.

Most landscapes of Australia are flat and dry.

Climate, plants and animals

Climate

Australia is well known for being a warm, sunny land. The northern third of the continent lies in the **tropical** zone, near the Earth's **equator**, where temperatures are warm to hot throughout the year.

The southern part of Australia lies in the **temperate** zone. Here the weather can be much cooler. During the winter, snow falls on the mountains in Australia's south-east, while rain falls on the coastal areas. Even deserts in the temperate zone can get cold and frosty during the winter months. However, southern Australia also has plenty of mild and sunny weather – even in winter – and temperatures during the summer months can be as warm as tropical temperatures. Australians are able to grow crops and enjoy outdoor recreation all year round. Droughts, floods and bushfires are common natural disasters, and can also occur any time of the year.

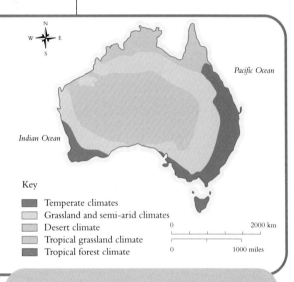

Pacific Ocean

Indian Ocean

Key
- Temperate climates
- Grassland and semi-arid climates
- Desert climate
- Tropical grassland climate
- Tropical forest climate

0   2000 km

0   1000 miles

Australia has plenty of sunny weather.

Wattles and eucalypts

There are two plants that are common throughout Australia: wattles and eucalypts. Both have **evergreen foliage**, and sometimes colourful flowers. The wattle is depicted on Australia's national coat of arms. Eucalypts have leaves and bark that can burn very easily, spreading bushfires in warm, dry weather.

Unique animals

Australia is an island continent, and its animals have been isolated from the rest of the world for millions of years. Many Australian animals are found nowhere else.

Australia has more **marsupials** and **monotremes** than any other region. Marsupials are pouched mammals, including kangaroos, wallabies, koalas, possums and wombats. Monotremes – the platypus and the echidna – are the only mammals that lay eggs.

Birds and reptiles

Many Australian birds, such as the black swan and the large flightless emu are also unique. There are also many kinds of colourful parrots, cockatoos, rosellas, budgerigars and lorikeets.

The warm weather of Australia suits many kinds of reptiles, including snakes, lizards, turtles and crocodiles. Australia has some of the largest lizards and most venomous snakes in the world.

Introduced animals

Some wild animals do not belong in Australia. These animals were brought to Australia by Europeans. Rabbits, foxes, goats, pigs, horses, cattle, cats, dogs, camels and cane toads are examples of introduced animals. They are not harmful in their natural environments, but when they run wild in Australia they cause great harm – preying on native animals or eating or trampling the native plants.

Grasslands and open woodlands
- red kangaroo
- grey kangaroo
- hairy-nosed wombat
- echidna
- brown snake
- goanna
- frilled-neck lizard
- bearded dragon
- emu
- mallee fowl
- wedge-tailed eagle
- galah
- kookaburra
- funnel-web spider

Deserts
- dingo
- wallaroo
- bilby
- desert rat-kangaroo
- marsupial mole
- mulga parrot
- sandswimming skink
- mountain devil
- death adder
- waterholding frog
- desert wolf spider

Temperate forests
- Tasmanian devil
- native cat
- koala
- ring-tailed possum
- sugar glider
- platypus
- common wombat
- lyrebird
- tawny frogmouth

Tropical forests
- tree kangaroo
- flying fox
- spotted cuscus
- cassowary
- bower bird
- Atlas moth

The kangaroo is one of Australia's many unique animals.

History and culture

The first people in Australia came from prehistoric Papua New Guinea and the islands of Indonesia, more than 40 000 years ago. The earliest societies were those of Aboriginal people and Torres Strait Islanders. Aboriginal people covered the widest area of Australia, spreading across the entire continent. Different Aboriginal groups lived in desert, mountain, forest and coastal environments. These groups were nomadic, constantly travelling from camp to camp, hunting and gathering food in different places. Torres Strait Islanders always lived close to the sea. They made their living by fishing, hunting, trading and farming.

Convict settlers

Australia was not settled by Europeans until 1788. Most of the earliest settlers were convicts and soldiers from England. They lived mainly on the east coast, and did not travel far from the shore. By the early 1800s, there were major cities in South Australia and Western Australia, and the settlers were pushing further into inland Australia, establishing more farms and towns. The land was used for wheat, sheep and wool, and beef and dairy cattle. The Aboriginal people were being steadily pushed off their land. Fighting sometimes broke out between Aboriginal and settler groups.

Some Aboriginal groups live in their traditional ways and speak their traditional languages.

Mineral wealth

Gold was discovered in eastern Australia during the mid-1800s. The gold rush that followed attracted hundreds of thousands of new settlers to the continent, and many new towns and cities sprang up near the goldfields. Even after the gold rush ended, discoveries of uranium, iron ore, silver, bauxite, nickel and petroleum made Australia an important mining country in the 1900s.

Australia today

Although Australia lies in the Asian region of the world, most of the people have an English-speaking European background. Their culture is similar to that of the UK, the USA and New Zealand. The **standard of living** is generally high, with a relaxed lifestyle. There have never been any major wars or **famines** in Australia. Families are not as closely tied as they are in Asia. It is not unusual for people to take jobs, go to schools or settle in homes that are hundreds of kilometres away from their parents.

Facts about living in Australia

- Australia has good schools and hospitals, as well as excellent transportation and communication systems.
- Along with farming and mining, tourism has become an important Australian industry.
- Not all Australians belong to an English-speaking European culture. Some Aboriginal groups live in their traditional ways and speak their traditional languages. Many immigrants speak another language, such as Turkish or Vietnamese.
- More than four out of every five Australians live in a city area.
- Most Australians belong to Christian religions (but do not regularly attend church).

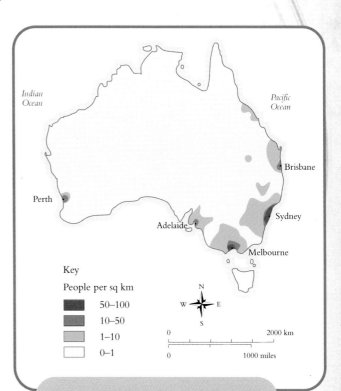

Key

People per sq km

- 50–100
- 10–50
- 1–10
- 0–1

Most Australians live near the coast, especially in the south-eastern corner of the continent.

Introducing
ANTARCTICA

Antarctica is the fifth-largest of the seven continents. It is the Earth's most southerly continent, lying over the South Pole. Antarctica is a harsh land. Of all the continents, it is the coldest, stormiest, windiest and iciest.

The name 'Antarctica' comes from the Greek word *antartik*, which means 'opposite the arctic' (since the Antarctic region lies opposite the arctic region around the North Pole). Antarctica is colder than the arctic region. Antarctica is so cold that few plants and animals can survive on the land. This means that most of the continent is a desert – a cold desert – with landscapes covered by ice, snow or bare rock. Antarctica has some amazing scenery, including ice cliffs, towering mountains, active volcanoes and the world's longest **glaciers**.

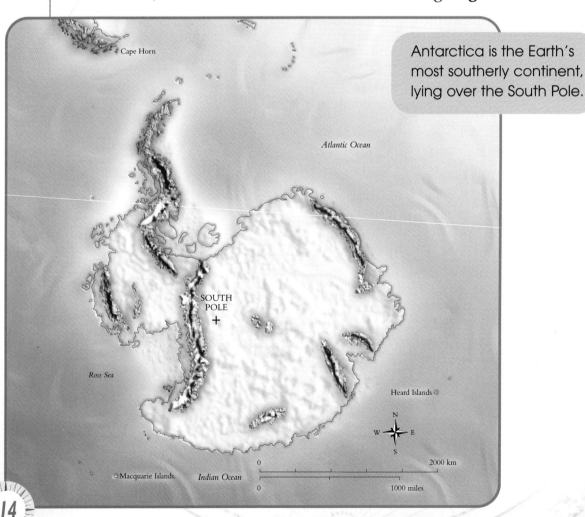

Cape Horn

Atlantic Ocean

> Antarctica is the Earth's most southerly continent, lying over the South Pole.

SOUTH POLE
+

Ross Sea

Heard Islands

N
W   E
S

0   2000 km

Macquarie Islands   Indian Ocean

0   1000 miles

Antarctica: facts and figures

Area: 14 000 000 sq km

Climate: polar

Population: no permanent residents

Highest peak: Vinson Massif (5140 metres above sea level)

Lowest point: Bentley Subglacial Trench (2538 metres below sea level)

Thickest ice: 4800 metres

Longest glacier: Lambert Glacier (700 km)

Products: fish, krill

Antarctica was the last continent to be discovered and explored. It is still the only continent with no permanent human residents. However, hundreds of scientists from many countries are stationed there to study glaciers, rocks, plants, animals or weather. Increasing numbers of tourists also visit Antarctica to see its wonders.

Most of the world's ice is found on the Antarctic continent.

Land and landforms

Almost all of the Antarctic continent is covered by thick layers of ice. Some of this ice has piled up higher than mountains or spread out into the sea. In fact, there is so much ice that it adds a great deal to the continent's size and height. If not for the ice, Antarctica would be the smallest continent.

The Antarctic icecap

The vast covering of ice over most of Antarctica is called an icecap or ice sheet. The Antarctic icecap has buried many of the continent's landforms, including hills, mountains, valleys, plains and lake beds. In some places, the icecap is more than four kilometres thick.

Glaciers

Antarctica has many **glaciers**. These are masses of ice that move downhill, towards the sea. Glaciers move more slowly than water, but they are very powerful, picking up rocks, scraping them against the ground, carving away mountains and bulldozing the land flat. When a glacier meets the sea, it can break up and form **icebergs**. Large icebergs can float for years in the sea before they finally melt.

Canada Glacier

Ice shelves

Along some parts of the Antarctic coastline the icecap reaches out over the water. This forms a large floating sheet of ice called an ice shelf. Ice shelves can cover thousands of square kilometres of water (the Ross Ice Shelf covers an area almost as large as France). On the outer edge of an ice shelf, great cliffs of ice tower over the sea, hundreds of metres high, making it difficult for ships to land. The outer parts of an ice shelf often break away to form wide, flat icebergs.

Mountains and valleys

Not all of Antarctica is covered with ice. Some mountain peaks stick out above the icecap. Antarctica's longest chain of mountains are the Transantarctic Mountains, which cross the entire continent. Transantarctic peaks can reach more than 4300 metres high. The region of the Transantarctic Mountains has some large areas that are not covered by ice. These areas are called dry valleys. Dry valleys are mainly covered by bare rock instead of ice. However, there are some lakes in dry valleys, and these are permanently covered by ice more than three metres deep.

Diary of a continent

▶ **200 million years ago**
Antarctica is part of the Gondwana supercontinent, along with Australia, Africa and South America.

▶ **150 million years ago**
Gondwana breaks up.

▶ **40 million years ago**
Antarctica breaks away from Australia, and drifts closer to the South Pole.

▶ **10 million years ago**
Antarctica grows very cold, with huge glaciers forming.

▶ **5 million years ago**
Most of the continent is covered with ice. Its land animals die out.

▶ **1820**
Antarctica is first sighted by ship.

▶ **1911**
Roald Amundsen becomes the first person to reach the South Pole.

Mt Erebus, on Ross Island, is the world's southernmost active volcano.

17

Climate, plants and animals

Climate

Temperatures are always cold in Antarctica. The coldest region of the continent is the inland, where winter temperatures have been recorded below –80° Celsius. The inland is also the driest region of Antarctica, with no rain and little snowfall. Coastal areas are milder, with some rain and summers that are warm enough to melt and clear the ice in certain areas. However, even here the temperatures are still cold. Only on some of the islands do summer temperatures normally rise above 0° Celsius. Antarctica is not only cold, but very windy. Blizzards are common and gusts can exceed 300 kilometres per hour. The wind makes temperatures seem much colder.

Lichen growing on bare rocks.

Hardy plants

Only small, hardy plants, such as grass or mosses, can survive in Antarctica. They grow mainly along ice-free parts of the coast. There are also **lichen** and algae, which can survive in much colder regions. Lichen can grow in the cracks of inland rocks and algae can grow in snow and ice.

Swimmers and fliers

Like most Antarctic plants, animals of this continent live near the coast or on islands. The only animals that live permanently on land are small **invertebrates** such as **midges** and flies. Most of the larger animals swim or fly, and get their main food supply from the sea. Some of them **migrate** to warmer areas during the winter. These animals include seals, penguins, cormorants, gulls, skuas and terns. Most of them eat fish, although some of them prey on

Antarctic seals have thick layers of fat to keep them warm.

other birds or seals. All these animals have layers of fat, fur or feathers on their bodies to keep them warm. **Parasites** such as lice, mites and ticks often keep warm by living on birds or seals.

Marine animals

Life is abundant in Antarctic seas. The most common marine animal is **krill**, a tiny shrimp-like creature that moves through the water in huge swarms. Many other marine animals feed on krill, and tonnes are caught and sold as food for people. Other Antarctic marine animals are squid, fish and a variety of whales.

Land and sea
- leopard seal
- southern elephant seal
- Weddell seal
- Ross seal
- crabeater seal
- Antarctic fur seal
- Adélie penguin
- emperor penguin
- chinstrap penguin
- gentoo penguin
- king penguin
- macaroni penguin

Air, land and sea
- wandering albatross
- Antarctic petrel
- giant petrel
- snow petrel
- storm petrel
- Cape pigeon
- southern fulmar
- brown skua
- sheathbill
- Dominican gull
- Antarctic tern

Antarctic ocean
- sperm whale
- killer whale
- southern bottlenose whale
- southern fourtooth whale
- blue whale
- fin whale
- humpback whale
- minke whale
- right whale
- sei whale
- icefish
- plunderfish
- Antarctic cod
- squid
- krill

Wandering albatross on Albatross Island, South Georgia.

19

Discovery and exploration

People knew about Antarctica long before it was discovered. Ancient Greek thinkers reasoned that there was a great **landmass** on the southern extreme of the Earth, but they could not agree what it was like. No one could prove Antarctica existed until 1820, when ships finally drew near enough to sight it. The first people to set foot on the continent were probably sealers or whalers. They were followed by explorers from many countries, including England, Australia and the USA. Early explorations of Antarctica occurred along its coastline. Serious exploration of the inland began in 1901, when a great race began to see who could reach the South Pole first.

Reaching the South Pole

Conditions were harsh and dangerous for early Antarctic explorers. With no modern transport and little protection from the cold, they had to face the dangers of **frostbite**, blizzards and treacherous **terrain**. In December 1911, two exploring parties began to close in on the South Pole. One was a British party led by Robert F. Scott. The other was a Norwegian party led by Roald Amundsen. Amundsen's party was travelling more efficiently and won the race on 14 December 1911. Scott's party did not reach the South Pole until 25 January 1912. Although Amundsen returned safely to the coast, Scott's entire party perished on their return trip, trapped by a blizzard between food supply stations. A research station at the South Pole has been named after the two parties' leaders – the Amundsen-Scott base.

Research stations

Antarctica today is mainly used for scientific purposes. The continent has no real towns or cities, but it does have more than 30 research stations, including one over the South Pole. These research stations house scientists, pilots and technicians – sometimes hundreds of them. No one lives at the stations permanently. They are maintained by countries including the UK, Australia, New Zealand, Argentina, Russia and the USA.

Some of these countries have claimed large regions of Antarctica as part of their territory. Even so, relations between different countries on Antarctica are open and friendly, without strict border patrols. The countries have agreed to keep military conflict and nuclear weapons out of Antarctica, not to undertake mining and to try to protect the native plants and animals.

Facts about living in **Antarctica**

- Many places on Antarctica are named after its early explorers, such as the Ross Ice Shelf, the Ellsworth Mountains and the Amundsen-Scott base at the South Pole.

- Antarctic research stations are maintained throughout the year. They are most crowded during the summer. The largest is McMurdo Station, which can have a summer population of 1000.

- No mining takes place in Antarctica, although petroleum, coal and other valuable minerals can be found there.

- A limited amount of fishing is allowed in Antarctic seas.

British researchers collecting data from Lake Druzhby near Davis Station.

This map shows where the permanent Antarctic research stations are located.

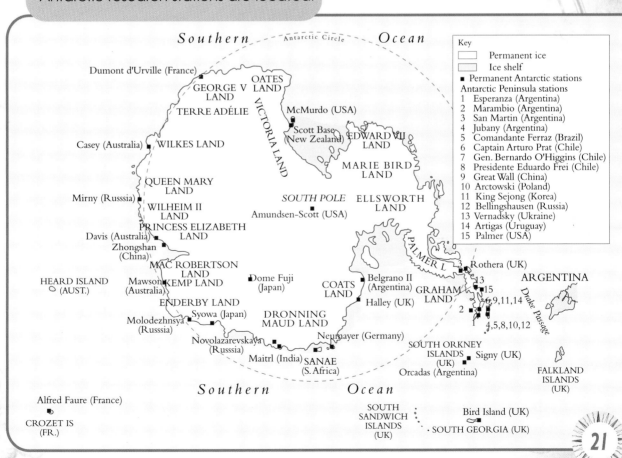

Southern   Antarctic Circle   Ocean

Key
- Permanent ice
- Ice shelf
- ■ Permanent Antarctic stations

Antarctic Peninsula stations
1. Esperanza (Argentina)
2. Marambio (Argentina)
3. San Martin (Argentina)
4. Jubany (Argentina)
5. Comandante Ferraz (Brazil)
6. Captain Arturo Prat (Chile)
7. Gen. Bernardo O'Higgins (Chile)
8. Presidente Eduardo Frei (Chile)
9. Great Wall (China)
10. Arctowski (Poland)
11. King Sejong (Korea)
12. Bellingshausen (Russia)
13. Vernadsky (Ukraine)
14. Artigas (Uruguay)
15. Palmer (USA)

Dumont d'Urville (France)
OATES LAND
GEORGE V LAND
TERRE ADÉLIE
VICTORIA LAND
McMurdo (USA)
Scott Base (New Zealand)
EDWARD VII LAND
Casey (Australia) WILKES LAND
MARIE BIRD LAND
QUEEN MARY LAND
Mirny (Russsia)
WILHEIM II LAND
SOUTH POLE
Amundsen-Scott (USA)
ELLSWORTH LAND
PRINCESS ELIZABETH LAND
Davis (Australia)
Zhongshan (China)
MAC ROBERTSON LAND
HEARD ISLAND (AUST.)
Mawson (Australia) KEMP LAND
Dome Fuji (Japan)
COATS LAND
Belgrano II (Argentina)
Halley (UK)
PALMER L.
Rothera (UK)
GRAHAM LAND
ARGENTINA
ENDERBY LAND
Syowa (Japan)
DRONNING MAUD LAND
Neumayer (Germany)
Drake Passage
2
15
4,5,8,10,12
6,9,11,14
1
3
13
Molodezhnsya (Russsia)
Novolazarevskaya (Russsia)
Maitrl (India)
SANAE (S. Africa)
SOUTH ORKNEY ISLANDS (UK)
Signy (UK)
Orcadas (Argentina)
FALKLAND ISLANDS (UK)

Southern   Ocean

Alfred Faure (France)
CROZET IS (FR.)
SOUTH SANDWICH ISLANDS (UK)
Bird Island (UK)
SOUTH GEORGIA (UK)

The making of
ISLAND CONTINENTS

As we know, Australia and Antarctica are island continents. Because they are island continents, they are isolated from other continents. This makes it difficult for plants, animals and people from other continents to cross over into the island continents. Australia and Antarctica are the only island continents today, but this was not always so. Every continent has been an island continent during some period in prehistoric time. For example, around 30 million years ago, South America was also an island continent.

Before Australia and Antarctica became island continents, they were joined to the ancient supercontinent of Gondwana. Africa and South America were also joined with Gondwana, and all four continents shared the same kinds of wildlife. What caused these continents to join together? What caused them to break apart? These questions puzzled scientists for many years. They finally found the answers in the last century.

Long ago, southern Tasmania was connected to Antarctica. Moving tectonic plates split these regions apart about 40 million years ago.

Plates in motion

Giant plates

Before the mid-1900s, most people had a false idea about the continents. They believed that the continents stood motionless in the Earth, in the same place for billions of years. Yet about 50 years ago, scientists discovered that the continents were moving. In fact, they have moved thousands of kilometres during ancient times, and are still moving today.

Around the 1960s, scientists discovered that the continents are attached to huge plates of rock, called **tectonic** plates. Together, the different plates make up the entire solid surface of the Earth, fitting together like a gigantic jigsaw puzzle. Many plates are larger than the continents, because they contain vast sections of the Earth's **crust**, including the ocean floor. Despite their large size, tectonic plates move very slowly over the Earth, but can cover great distances over millions of years. The way the continents move is called plate tectonics. Plate tectonics helps us understand the changing position of continents, and how island continents form.

Tectonic plates are made up of rock from the crust and the upper **mantle**. Each plate is about 100 kilometres thick. The rigid plates float on the layer of rocks below, moving sideways along the hot lower surface. When the plates move, anything attached to them moves as well, including continents and parts of the ocean floor. This movement is extremely slow – about 10 centimetres every year – but the plates can cover great distances over millions of years.

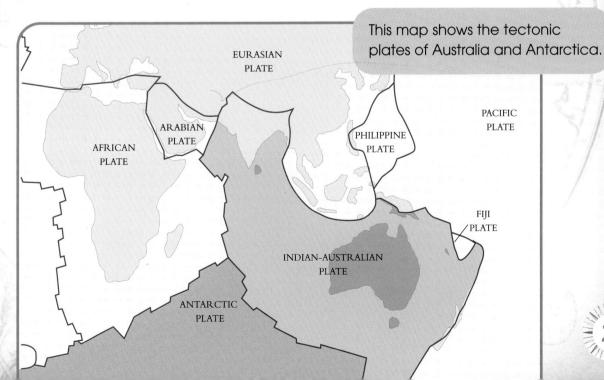

This map shows the tectonic plates of Australia and Antarctica.

EURASIAN PLATE

ARABIAN PLATE

AFRICAN PLATE

PHILIPPINE PLATE

PACIFIC PLATE

FIJI PLATE

INDIAN-AUSTRALIAN PLATE

ANTARCTIC PLATE

Plate tectonics helps us understand how the continents slowly move across the Earth's surface. When the plates carry two continents towards each other, they may eventually connect with each other. When the plates carry the continents apart, island continents are more likely to form.

Pangaea

Australia and Antarctica were not island continents about 250 million years ago. In fact, there were no island continents anywhere on Earth. All of the continents were pushed together into a giant supercontinent called Pangaea (pronounced *pan-jee-uh*; the name comes from two Greek words meaning 'all land'). At this time, Gondwana existed, but not as a separate supercontinent. It formed the southern part of Pangaea. Gondwana was made up of five great **landmasses** – Australia, Antarctica, Africa, South America and India. Europe, Asia and North America were joined together to make up the northern section of Pangaea, called Laurasia.

Regional differences

The regions of Gondwana and Laurasia were different from each other in many ways. Gondwana had many widespread forms of prehistoric plants and animals that were not found in most of Laurasia, such as *Lystrosaurus* (a hippopotamus-like reptile) and *Glossopteris* (a plant with tongue-shaped leaves). Even the **climate** of these two regions was different. For millions of years, much of Laurasia lay in the Earth's warm, **tropical** zone. At the same time, much of Gondwana lay closer to the freezing South Pole, covered by huge glaciers.

250–200 million years ago

130–100 million years ago

70–40 million years ago

The Earth's continents were once pushed together into a giant supercontinent called Pangaea.

Today's continents

Break-up and isolation

By 200 million years ago, the plates below Pangaea began to break it apart. Laurasia and Gondwana became two smaller supercontinents. Australia was getting more isolated at this time, lying in a very remote part of Gondwana. Antarctica still had a more central position, very close to the other Gondwana continents. By 150 million years ago, Gondwana and Laurasia were breaking up into the single continents we know today. However, Australia and Antarctica remained connected for a long time. They finally separated and became island continents about 40 million years ago.

When continents break apart from each other, they may become island continents. But they do not always stay that way. When Africa and South America broke away from the other Gondwana continents, they drifted towards the northern continents. Millions of years later, South America joined to North America, and Africa joined to Asia. India was another Gondwana landmass that drifted north, eventually joining with Asia. Although India is not recognised as a separate continent, it is often called a **subcontinent**.

A **fossil** of *Glossopteris*, an ancient plant with tongue-shaped leaves, which was a common plant on the Gondwana supercontinent.

Lystrosaurus was a hippo-shaped reptile of ancient Gondwana.

Changes in
CLIMATE

The movement of **tectonic** plates has changed Australia and Antarctica many times over the past 300 million years. These two continents have been joined to each other, then pushed into a supercontinent, then split into island continents.

As a continent changes position, other changes can occur as well, such as changes in **climate**. For example, if a continent in the **temperate** zone drifts into a **tropical** zone, the climate will grow much warmer. Of course, not all changes in climate are caused by a continent's movement. Some climate changes are global, and affect large parts of the Earth. This happened during the last **ice age**, when world temperatures became much colder.

Different directions

Gondwana had completely broken up about 60 million years ago. However, Australia and Antarctica were still joined together deep in the Southern Hemisphere. Both continents shared the same kinds of birds, reptiles, **amphibians**, small mammals and freshwater fish. Both continents had the same wet climate, with large areas of shady rainforest. By 30 million years ago, Australia and Antarctica had finally split apart. Although they still shared many of the same kinds of plants and animals, these two island continents were moving in different directions. Australia began drifting north. Antarctica drifted deeper into the Southern Hemisphere.

Temperate rainforests, similar to those of north-eastern Tasmania, once covered much of Australia and Antarctica.

By five million years ago, Australia's climate became mainly warm and dry. Most of the rainforest plants and animals had disappeared. They were replaced by woodland, grassland and desert wildlife. During the Ice Age, which began about two million years ago, Australia's climate became colder for a while. **Glaciers** developed in the southern part of the continent. But when the Ice Age ended, the glaciers vanished, and most of the continent became warm and dry again.

Something very different happened to Antarctica. Antarctica drifted further into the South Polar region. Glaciers began to grow on the South Pole after Antarctica broke away from Australia and, by 10 million years ago, they formed a thick icecap over much of the continent. By five million years ago, it was too cold for most of the plants and animals to survive on land, and nearly all of the continent became buried in ice.

Australia and Antarctica are still being moved by tectonic plates. Both continents are likely to drift north. Fifty million years from now Australia will be much closer to the **equator**, maybe even linked with Asia. Heavy rain will fall over a wider area of the Australian continent. Huge desert regions will turn into rainforests again. The Antarctic climate will go through even more drastic changes as this continent drifts north. One hundred and eighty million years from now, the Antarctic icecap will melt, rivers will flow and the land will again be occupied by a wide variety of plants and animals.

Australia's climate became mainly warm and dry around five million years ago.

Isolation and WILDLIFE

When Australia and Antarctica were part of Pangaea, they shared the same kinds of wildlife with all other continents. However, after becoming island continents, they developed different kinds of plants and animals. This happened during the **Age of Mammals**, a time when large and small mammals became common throughout the world. Many different kinds of mammals became widespread at this time, including prehistoric cats, bears, elephants, horses, camels and deer. But none of these large land mammals inhabited Australia or Antarctica. They had no way of reaching these isolated continents.

Ancient marsupials

Ancient Australia was inhabited by a wide variety of **marsupials** (pouched mammals). They included giant kangaroos and wombats and a huge lumbering creature called *Diprotodon*. Although these giants are now extinct, many of the more familiar marsupials still survive. There are also some mammals without pouches – including seals, bats, mice and dingoes – that managed to enter Australia.

Ancient *Diprotodon* was the largest marsupial ever to live.

Cold-weather animals

Prehistoric animals that lived in Antarctica were also isolated from other continents. But even if animals from other continents could have somehow reached Antarctica, most kinds would have died out from the cold. Only animals such as seals, penguins and small insects could survive the freezing weather.

End of isolation

Australia and Antarctica are still island continents. However, since the arrival of Europeans, they are no longer so isolated. European animals have been brought into these continents, sometimes causing great harm to the native wildlife. People have hunted the lands of Australia and fished the seas of both continents. There are also problems from pollution.

Protecting wildlife

Today, there is more pressure to preserve the wildlife of the island continents. Many Australian native plants and animals are now protected by law, and there are more national parks and nature reserves where wildlife cannot be hunted. There are also strict laws controlling the kinds of plants and animals that can be brought into the country. Environmental groups from all over the world are concerned about Antarctica. They put pressure on governments to ban whale hunting and too much fishing in the seas. They also want a guarantee that the continent will never be used for mining or military activity.

Changing attitudes

Australia's first European settlers did not appreciate the continent's unique plants and animals. They cut down many of the native eucalypts and wattles and replaced them with European trees, including oak, willow and poplar. They killed many of the marsupials (causing some to become extinct) and allowed European animals to overrun the land. These settlers actually wanted to destroy the native plants and animals and turn Australia into a country like England or Scotland. Today, however, people living in Australia take more pride in their continent's unique wildlife.

Community tree planting in Australia. Australians take pride in their unique plants and animals.

GLOSSARY

Age of Mammals   a time in Earth's history when mammals became the largest animals (about 65 million years ago to recent times)

Age of Reptiles   a time in Earth's history when reptiles became the largest animals (about 250–65 million years ago)

alpine   in a high mountain region

amphibians   four-legged animals that lay eggs in water, such as frogs

climate   the kind of weather that occurs in a particular region

crust   the Earth's outermost layer of rock, about 8–70 kilometres thick

elevation   height above sea level

equator   an imaginary line around the middle of the Earth's surface

erosion   the way landscape surfaces are naturally worn away. Erosion can be caused by water, wind or ice.

evergreen foliage   leaves or needles of a plant that stay green all the time, such as that of pines, wattles or eucalypts

famine   a severe shortage of food in a place

fertile   rich in nutrients

frostbite   an injury caused by exposure of the skin to extreme cold

geographers   people who study geography, the study of the Earth's surface

glaciers   masses of ice that move slowly across the land

ice age   a time when parts of the Earth became colder and were covered by glaciers. There have been many ice ages in ancient history.

icebergs   masses of floating ice

invertebrates   types of animals that do not have backbones, such as spiders

krill   small, shrimp-like animals of the ocean

land bridge   an area of land that connects two continents

landmass   a large area of land, such as a continent

lichen   a plant-like form of life that can grow on rock or wood, and needs little moisture to survive

livestock   farm animals, such as cattle, pigs and chickens

mantle   the layer of very dense rock (about 2900 kilometres thick) below the Earth's crust

marsupials   mammals that carry their young in a pouch

midges   kinds of very small insects

migrate   to move from one area to another

monotremes   mammals that lay eggs

Northern Hemisphere   the northern half of the Earth between the North Pole and the equator

parasites   living things that dwell on, or in, a plant or animal and take nourishment from it

pharmaceuticals   drugs or medicines

polar   of the arctic or Antarctic regions

Southern Hemisphere   the southern half of the Earth between the South Pole and the equator

standard of living   the level of goods and income enjoyed by a society

subcontinent   a large landmass that forms a section of a continent

tectonic   relating to the structure and changes in the Earth's crust

temperate   moderate; not permanently hot or cold. Temperate climates are those with temperate characteristics, such as a Mediterranean or a cool temperate climate.

terrain   a section of land, especially with reference to its natural features

timber   trees or forested land; wood useful for constructing buildings, furniture and wooden objects

tropical   of the tropics, the warm regions around the equator

FURTHER INFORMATION

Websites

About Geography   **http://geography.about.com**
Includes sites for world atlas and maps, glossary, quizzes and homework help.

National Geographic   **www.nationalgeographic.com**
Includes sites for travel, maps, nature, history and culture.

Books

Lands and Peoples. Grolier Incorporated, Danbury, 1995.

The Usborne-Internet-Linked Encyclopedia of World Geography. Usborne Publishing Ltd, London, 2001.

INDEX